BODY SYSTEMS

Eating and Digestion

Angela Royston

Heinemann

First published in Great Britain by Heinemann Library
Halley Court, Jordan Hill, Oxford OX2 8EJ
a division of Reed Educational and Professional Publishing Ltd.

OXFORD FLORENCE PRAGUE MADRID ATHENS MELBOURNE
AUCKLAND KUALA LUMPUR SINGAPORE TOKYO IBADAN
NAIROBI KAMPALA JOHANNESBURG GABORONE
PORTSMOUTH NH (USA) CHICAGO MEXICO CITY SAO PAULO

Designed by Inklines and Small House Design
Illustrations by David Cook, except: Peter Stevenson, p.17; Peter Bull Art
Studio, p.11, p.15 (left), p.16 & p.21; John Bovosier, p.12 & p.13.

Printed in Great Britain by Bath Press Colourbooks, Glasgow
Originated in Great Britain by Dot Gradations, Wickford

01 00 99 98 97
10 9 8 7 6 5 4 3 2 1

ISBN 0 431 06205 6
This title is also available in a hardback library edition (ISBN 0 431 06204 8).

British Library Cataloguing in Publication Data
Royston, Angela
    Eating & digestion. – (Body systems)
    1. Ingestion – Juvenile literature 2. Digestion – Juvenile literature
    I. Title
    612.3

Acknowledgements
The Publishers would like to thank the following for permission to reproduce
photographs:
Colorific: p.29; Oxford Scientific Films: p.5; Science Photo Library: p.9 (right),
p.18, p.21, p.22, p.23, p.24–5, p.25 (right), p.27 (both); Telegraph Colour
Library: p.8–9, p.28–9; Tony Stone Images: p.4, p.7, p.14.

Commissioned photographs p.6 & p.13: Trevor Clifford.
Cover photograph: Trevor Clifford.

Our thanks to Yvonne Hewson and Dr Kath Hadfield for their comments in
the preparation of this book.

Every effort has been made to contact copyright holders of any material
reproduced in this book. Any omissions will be rectified in subsequent
printings if notice is given to the Publisher.

Contents

Eating to live

Your body is like a very complicated machine, and like many other machines it needs fuel to keep it going. Cars burn petrol to drive the engine and move the wheels. Our fuel is food. It gives us energy to move around, grow and stay healthy. Special parts of the body, which together make up the **digestive system**, turn the food you put in your mouth into the kind of fuel your body can use.

Digestive system

The process of **digestion** begins in your mouth. When you eat a sandwich, you first chew it with your teeth, then swallow it. It is pushed down to your **stomach**, where it churns around for two or three hours. It then passes into a long tube called the **intestines**.

The food is gradually broken down into smaller and smaller pieces and the good parts, which are called **nutrients**, are absorbed into your body. The rest winds its way along to the end of the tube and is finally forced out of your body when you go to the toilet.

► *This athlete drinks glucose and water to give him energy and liquid during a marathon run. He will certainly need plenty of energy to finish this 42-km race!*

Delivering the food

The nutrients pass into your blood and so are taken all over your body. Every part of the body is made up of tiny living **cells**. Most cells are too small to see without a magnifying glass, but each one needs a supply of fuel in the form of food. Each kind of cell has a particular job to do. Some form bones, some form skin, and others form the **heart**. Each part of you is built up of millions of cells, including the parts that make the digestive system!

Did you know?

We need to eat a huge amount of food to stay alive and healthy. You could easily eat 78 kg of potatoes, 26 kg of sugar, 500 apples, 150 loaves of bread and over 200 eggs each year, not to mention all the pizzas, chocolate and other food. Most people in Europe, North America and Australasia probably eat about 35,000 kg of food during their lives – nearly 1000 times the weight of your body.

◄ *A drop of blood, magnified thousands of times to show the red blood cells. Blood is made of different kinds of cells. One of blood's many jobs is to take food to all the other living cells in the body.*

Food, glorious food

When you are hungry you may feel like eating a huge pizza with lots of toppings. Your eyes see cheese, tomato, mushroom and pepperoni but did you ever realize that your body is crying out for **carbohydrates** and **fats**, **proteins**, **vitamins** and **minerals**? You need proteins to grow and replace old, worn-out **cells**, carbohydrates and fats to give you energy, and vitamins and minerals to keep your body working properly.

Energy-rich food

We use most of our food to give us energy. Carbohydrates – bread, pasta, rice and potatoes – are the best source of energy. Sugar is a carbohydrate too. Weight for weight, fat gives more energy than any other food. The biggest source of fat in our food is meat, milk (including butter and cheese) and oil. Spreads made from, for example, sunflower oil, are also mainly fat. But be careful – don't eat more fat than you need.

Body-building

Meat, fish, eggs, cheese and beans all contain lots of proteins. These complicated substances help you grow. As you grow taller, your **muscles**, **lungs**, **heart** and so on have to grow bigger too. Your body cells do not live as long as you do. Most live only a few weeks before they die, but the body uses proteins to make a continuous supply of new cells to replace them.

▶ *A juicy pizza looks and smells delicious. It also contains different kinds of **nutrient** to give you energy, help you grow and keep your body healthy.*

6

Vitamins and minerals

Our food contains small amounts of vitamins and minerals. These chemicals help the cells to work properly. There are several kinds of vitamins and most are known simply by letters of the alphabet. Carrots, fish and sweet corn, for example, contain vitamin A, which helps the body fight disease. Eggs, Marmite and meat contain vitamin B, which every cell needs to work properly. Bones and teeth need the minerals calcium and phosphorus, and our blood needs iron.

◄ *Fresh fruit and vegetables are rich in vitamin C. This vitamin helps your skin to keep healthy and is essential to prevent a disease called scurvy, which causes bleeding in the gums, skin and joints.*

Did you know?

You use up energy even when you are asleep! Energy is measured in calories (cal) and you burn 55 cal every hour that you sleep. Sitting uses 75 cal/hr and walking 200 cal/hr. Climbing stairs burns 800 cal/hr, but could you do it for that long? To replace all that burnt-up energy you could eat a plate of spaghetti (400 cal), a portion of baked beans (178 cal), a packet of crisps (154 cal) and one or two oranges (40 cal).

Breaking down food

How does your body turn the food you eat into the **nutrients** it needs? The answer is it **digests** it – it breaks it down into smaller and smaller pieces. The digestive organs are so thorough that they can reduce food to **molecules** which dissolve in water and pass into the blood. Your body uses **digestive juices** and special **proteins**, called **enzymes**, to break down your food.

In the kitchen

Cooking food kills any germs in it. It can also help the process of digestion by breaking down the **cell** walls a little so that the food is easier to chew. But food needs to be heated to a high temperature (100 degrees centigrade – 100°C – or more) before it starts to cook. The human body is able to digest, or break down, food at much lower temperatures.

In the body

Acids in your mouth and **stomach** mix with the food and help to break it up. Enzymes are the magic ingredient that allows your body to digest food at about 37 °C, in other words, without cooking. They allow the **chemical reactions** that break down the food to take place. Acids in the stomach also kill off germs and **bacteria**. Later on in the digestive process, however, the body actually relies on other bacteria to break down still undigested food.

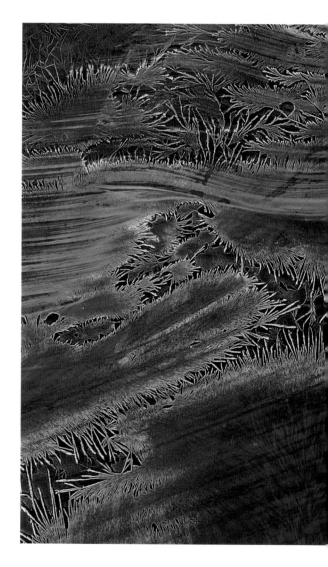

▲ *Acids are very powerful. This metal has been worn away and broken down by acid. In your stomach, acids work with enzymes to break down food.*

▲ This picture of an enzyme was drawn by a computer.

Did you know?

Our bodies are made of the same substances as our food, but the acids that help to break down food do not digest our own stomachs. This is because the stomach is protected by a thick coating of sticky mucus which shields it from the acidic digestive juices.

The digestion machine

The **digestive system** is a production line for processing food. As food travels from the mouth to the **anus**, it is churned, squeezed and squirted with various **digestive juices**. The main parts of the digestion machine are the mouth, the **oesophagus**, the **stomach**, the small **intestine** and the large intestine. The whole tube is called the **alimentary canal** and it is about 10 m long. Various **glands** keep it supplied with juices and **enzymes**.

Moving food along

The alimentary canal is made of **muscle** – not muscle like that in your arms and legs, but smooth muscle. Its main job is to push the food along. It does this rather like squeezing toothpaste from a tube. This is called **peristalsis**, and the wave-like movements of the muscle keep the food moving. This means that you can swallow even when you are standing on your head!

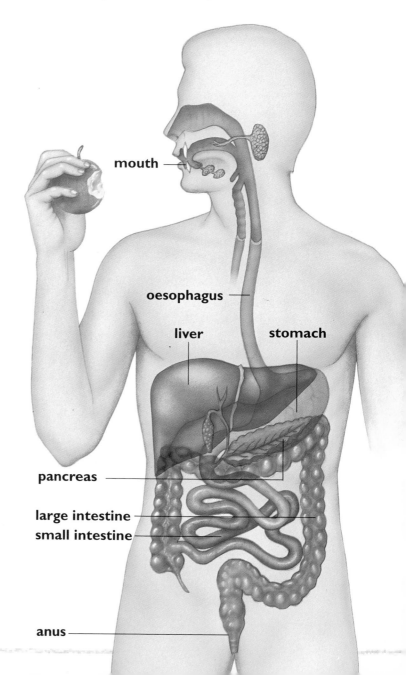

▶ *The main parts of the digestive system.*

mouth

oesophagus

liver

stomach

pancreas

large intestine

small intestine

anus

One-way gates

Where each part of the digestive system joins the next part, there is usually a kind of round **valve** called a **sphincter**. Valves are one-way gates. They make sure that food keeps going in the right direction. So, if you touch your toes, the food in your stomach will not come back up to your mouth. You can, of course, still be sick. The anus, at the end of the line, is also a sphincter. It controls when the waste food leaves your body.

Glands

There are glands placed all along the alimentary canal. They provide the different chemicals which are needed at each stage. The **liver** and the **pancreas** are both large glands. The stomach is lined with millions of tiny glands which make **acid** and enzymes.

▼ *The muscles of the intestines, or* **gut***, contract (shorten) and relax to push the food along.*

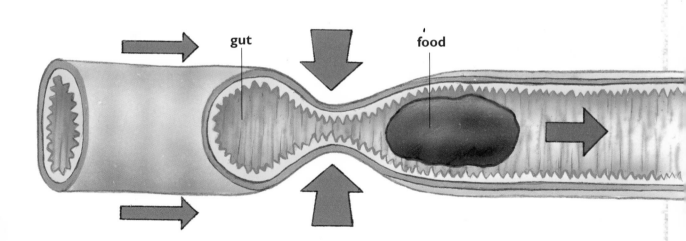

gut   food

Did you know?

It takes about a day for food to pass right through the alimentary canal. A few seconds after you swallow it, the food lands in your stomach where it stays for about three hours (longer for a big meal). It takes around another 20 hours to pass through the intestines. Some food is digested much faster than other kinds of food. On the other hand, food that is hard to digest, such as some nuts, may take two or three days to make the whole journey.

Taking a bite

The process of **digestion** begins in the mouth. Teeth break up
the food and grind it into smaller pieces. Only the lower jaw
can move, so the lower teeth work against the upper teeth to bite
and chew. Teeth have to be hard and tough to do this job.
They are covered with a layer of enamel – the hardest
substance in the body.

Mechanical breakers

Teeth are like precision tools –
shaped to do different jobs. You use
the incisors, the eight flat, sharp front
teeth, to take a bite or slice of food.
The four long canines, fang-like teeth
on each side of the front teeth, are
good for gripping and tearing.

The eight premolars tear and grind
the food, and twelve large flat molars
at the back of your mouth grind the
food down into small pieces. Adults
have 32 teeth altogether, but the first
set of teeth, the milk teeth, consist of
only 20.

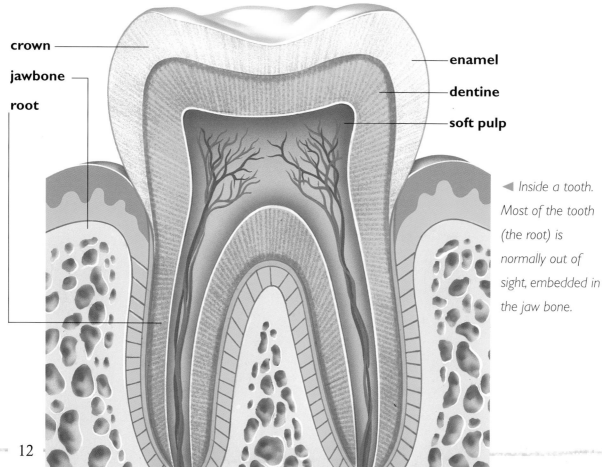

crown

jawbone

root

enamel

dentine

soft pulp

◄ *Inside a tooth.*
Most of the tooth
(the root) is
normally out of
sight, embedded in
the jaw bone.

Tooth decay

Even when you have swallowed, tiny particles of food are left in your mouth. They cling to your teeth and gums and cause decay. Sugar does the most damage.

Bacteria in the mouth change sugary food particles into **acids** which attack the teeth's enamel. First, small holes appear in the enamel, then larger ones in the dentine beneath. If the decay is allowed to reach the soft pulp in the centre, it will cause agonizing toothache. The only way to stop your teeth decaying is to brush them night and morning and always after eating sweet things.

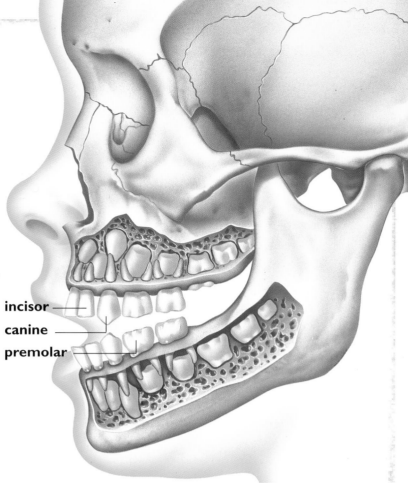

incisor

canine

premolar

▲ A person has two sets of teeth. The first set begins to fall out from about the age of six. Bigger, permanent teeth (shown in blue) push through the gum to take their place.

◀ To avoid tooth decay, you have to brush your teeth soon after eating sweet things.

Did you know?

George Washington, the first president of the United States of America, probably did not clean his teeth properly. They were so rotten his dentist pulled them out and made him a false set carved from a hippopotamus tusk. Celluloid, the first plastic, invented in 1868, was soon used to make false teeth. Unfortunately, the teeth melted when their wearer drank hot liquid!

In your mouth

The first thing you notice when you put something in your mouth is what it feels and tastes like. Rotten or poisonous food often tastes bad – a good warning not to eat it. Your tongue moves the food around your mouth and the process of **digestion** begins. As well as being broken down into smaller pieces by chewing, food has to be mixed with saliva (spit) to make it soft and mushy enough to be swallowed.

Tongue

The tongue is a big **muscle** which makes the mushy, chewed food into a ball ready for swallowing. The tongue is also mainly responsible for the sense of taste. The tip, edge and back are covered with about 3000 taste-buds, but there are just four different kinds of them. Every taste is a mixture of sweet, salty, sour and bitter. Each taste-bud reacts to just one of the four basic tastes and your brain learns to recognize the mixture.

Pure chocolate is very bitter. It is mixed with sugar to make it more tasty. But if you lick chocolate with just the tip of your tongue, all you will taste is sweetness. You have to push the chocolate to the back of your tongue to get the full flavour.

► *Licking an ice-cream quickly tells you how good it tastes.*

Saliva

Taste-buds do not react to dry food. It has to be mixed with saliva first. There are three pairs of salivary **glands** that supply the mouth. One pair makes the sticky liquid that mixes with the chewed food and two pairs make an **enzyme** that starts the chemical process of digestion. It turns some of the starch in **carbohydrates** into sugar. Saliva is also slightly **antiseptic,** so it attacks any germs that enter your mouth.

▼ Taste-buds are concentrated around the edge and back of the tongue. Each part of the tongue responds to a different kind of taste.

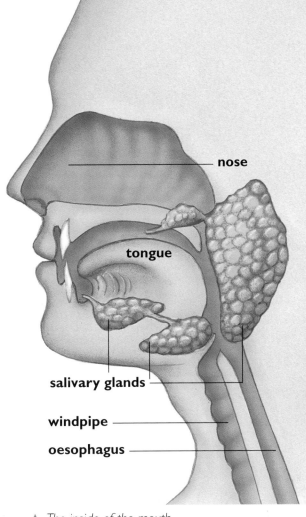

The inside of the mouth labels: nose, tongue, salivary glands, windpipe, oesophagus.

▲ The inside of the mouth.

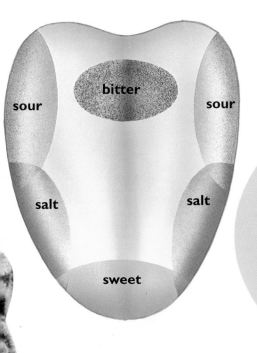

Tongue map labels: bitter, sour, sour, salt, salt, sweet.

Did you know?

You make over a litre of spit every day and you swallow it all the time. See how long you can last without swallowing – or dribbling. It won't be more than a minute or two. You make more saliva at some times than at others. When you see food you really want to eat, your mouth begins to 'water' with saliva, getting ready to eat. When your body needs more liquid, however, your mouth becomes dry and you feel thirsty.

Going down

When you have chewed a lump of food it becomes reduced to a small packet of mush called a **bolus**. Your tongue pushes it into your throat and you automatically swallow it. The bolus slides into the throat and down the **oesophagus**, helped along by **peristalsis**. The act of swallowing causes special flaps to close the passages into your nose and lungs so the only way the bolus can go is down to your **stomach**.

Swallowing

The roof of the mouth is called the **palate**. It is hard in the main cavity of the mouth but becomes soft at the back. As soon as a bolus of food touches the **pharynx** at the back of the throat you swallow automatically.

The soft palate moves up and closes the air passage from the nose. At the same time, a flap, called the **epiglottis**, closes the windpipe to the lungs. You cannot breathe for one or two seconds while you swallow.

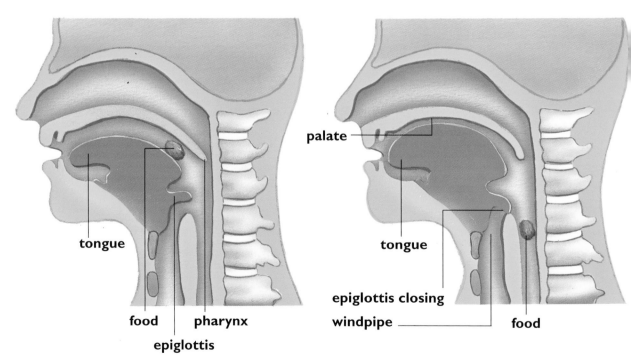

▲ As you swallow, the epiglottis closes
off the windpipe to stop you choking.

Choking

There are two causes of choking. Sometimes a large lump of food gets to the throat and you swallow it by mistake. Most such lumps slowly move down the oesophagus, and you can often feel them doing so. What if a fish bone or some other obstacle gets stuck in your throat?

It will usually be dislodged by coughing or when someone pats you on the back. Sometimes food 'goes down the wrong way'. The epiglottis has not done its job and a crumb or two has got into the windpipe. Again, coughing, spluttering and a pat on the back helps to clear the windpipe.

▲ Sometimes, swallowing can be hard work!

Did you know?

Some specially trained people take part in competitions to see who can drink the most liquid in the shortest time. Some even manage to drink over a litre in a few seconds. They achieve this feat by holding their throats in the swallowing position so they can pour the liquid straight into their stomachs. Do not try it yourself – you will almost certainly choke.

In your stomach

The **stomach** is a stretchy, muscular bag which both stores food and helps to **digest** it. It acts a bit like an electric liquidizer, churning the food around and turning it into a liquid, called **chyme**. The **valve** at the lower end of the stomach empties the chyme, bit by bit, into the small **intestine**. It takes about three hours for an ordinary meal to pass through the stomach. A very large meal can take up to six hours.

Food mixers

The wall of the stomach has three layers. Beneath the outer coat is a layer of **muscle** which contracts every few seconds and moves the food around.

The innermost layer, the stomach lining, is covered with tiny **glands.** Some secrete **mucus**, others secrete hydrochloric **acid** and **enzymes**. As soon as food reaches the stomach these **gastric juices** pour over it. Hydrochloric acid kills germs and mixes with the food. Enzymes begin to digest **protein**. Some sugar is absorbed into the blood, but the main process of digestion takes place in the small intestine.

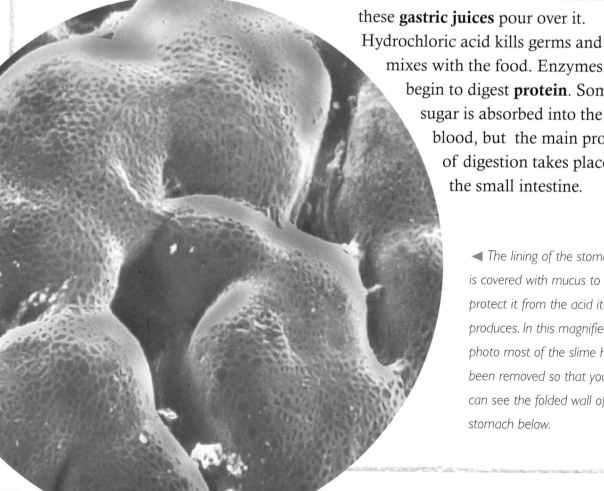

◀ *The lining of the stomach is covered with mucus to protect it from the acid it produces. In this magnified photo most of the slime has been removed so that you can see the folded wall of the stomach below.*

Vomiting

A number of things can make you sick, including bad smells, food which is too rich and sugary, and illness. Normally the valve between the **oesophagus** and the stomach allows food to drop into the stomach but prevents it going back up again.

When you are sick, however, the muscles in your belly and **diaphragm** squeeze your stomach, and the valve to the small intestine closes, so that the contents of the stomach are forced up the oesophagus and into your mouth.

► *The stomach is shaped roughly like a boxing glove. Bands of muscle squeeze it in different directions, churning up the food inside it. The inner lining is ridged and pitted.*

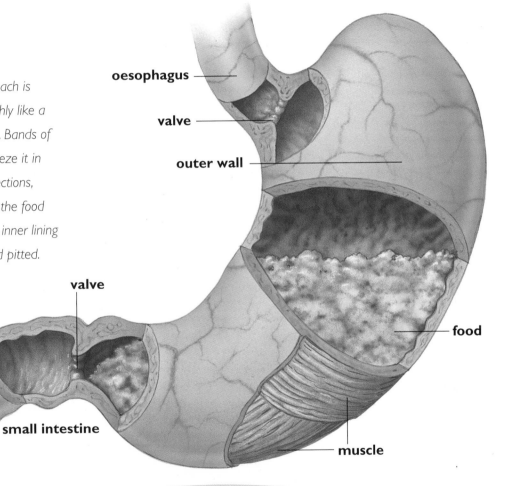

oesophagus

valve

outer wall

valve

small intestine

food

muscle

Did you know?

Do you sometimes have a hollow feeling in your stomach when you are hungry? The stomach is small when it is empty. As you eat, it stretches, perhaps to two or three times the volume, depending on how much you eat. Then you feel full. Our stomachs can hold up to a litre and a half – small compared to those of some animals. A cow's stomach can hold up to 180 litres, though it does have several sections!

In the small intestine

The small **intestine** is not actually small – it is about 7 m long and 3 cm wide. It has three parts. In the first part, called the **duodenum**, **digestive juices** break down the **chyme** into smaller **molecules** and neutralizes any **acids**. The breaking down continues in the middle part, the **jejunum**. By the time the molecules reach the third part, the **ileum,** they have become small enough to move through the thin walls of the **gut** into the blood.

Sprayed with juices

The duodenum is about 25 cm long. Its juices neutralize the acidic liquid that arrives from the **stomach**. About halfway along the duodenum, a tube from the **gall bladder** and one fom the **pancreas** join the duodenum. **Enzymes** and digestive juices from the pancreas continue the process of breaking down the **proteins** which started in the stomach. They also attack the **carbohydrates**. **Bile** from the gall bladder breaks down **fats**, in much the same way as washing-up liquid breaks down fat.

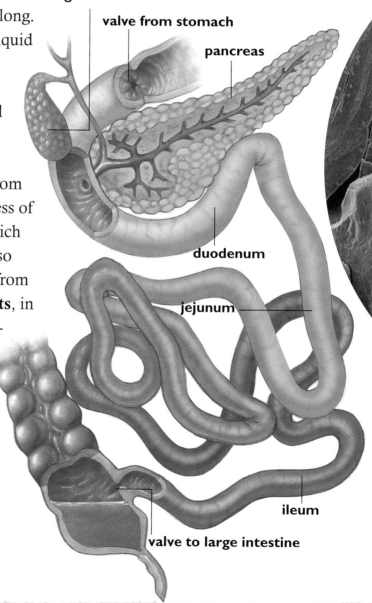

gall bladder

valve from stomach

pancreas

duodenum

jejunum

ileum

valve to large intestine

▶ *The long tube of the small intestine is coiled into the space between the ribs and the pelvis. Small quantities of chyme pass into the small intestine through a* **valve** *at the end of the stomach.*

Absorbed into the blood

Even seven hours after eating, very little food has actually been absorbed into the bloodstream. This happens mainly in the ileum. By this time proteins have been reduced to **amino acids**, carbohydrates to simple sugars and fats into tiny fatty molecules.

These are now small enough to pass between the **cells** of the **villi** and through the walls of the tiny blood vessels into the blood itself. But before your body cells can use this new supply of energy and **nutrients** they go to the **liver** for processing.

▼ The walls of the villi in the ileum are so thin, food molecules can pass through them into the bloodstream.

blood vessels

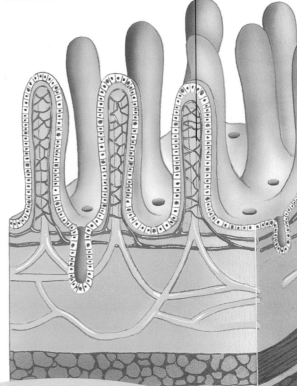

▲ The lining of the ileum is folded into tiny ridges covered with millions of tiny finger-like villi.

Did you know?

The small intestine is specially designed to provide an enormous surface through which food molecules can be absorbed. If you unravelled the entire tube, flattened out all the villi and straightened out all the ridges, you would get an area of lining large enough to cover a table-tennis table, an area five times as large as the area of skin on your body.

Liver and pancreas

The **liver** is the largest **organ** in your body. Together with a smaller organ, the **pancreas**, it helps your body to absorb food into the bloodstream. The liver weighs about 1.5 kg and carries out more than 500 different jobs.

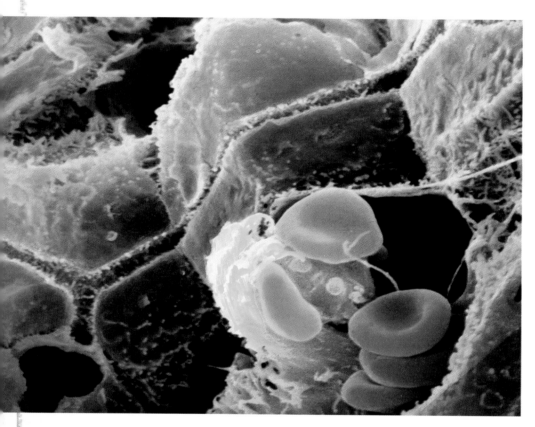

◄ This magnified photo shows the **cells** in the liver.

Processing food and waste

Blood, rich with **nutrients**, goes from the small **intestine** straight to the liver. If there is more **digested** food in the blood than the body needs, the liver changes the extra into glycogen, a kind of sugar, and stores it. It also stores some **vitamins** and destroys some poisons. It releases the right amount of nutrients into the blood.

The blood is then taken to the **heart** and **lungs** and, well stocked with food and oxygen, the blood is pumped to all the body's cells. The liver also cleans the blood. It removes dead red blood cells and waste products which have been produced by the cells. Some of the waste is made into **bile** and stored in the **gall bladder**.

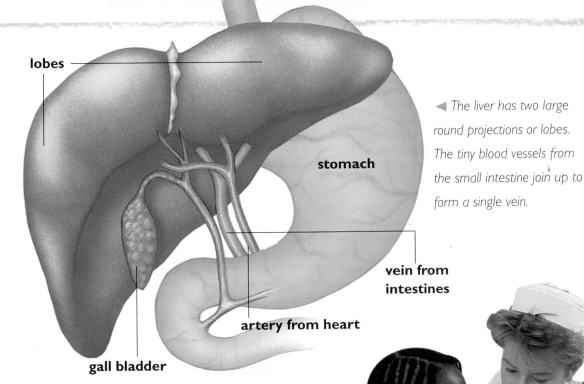

lobes

stomach

◄ The liver has two large round projections or lobes. The tiny blood vessels from the small intestine join up to form a single vein.

vein from intestines

artery from heart

gall bladder

The pancreas

The pancreas has two jobs. Every day it makes about a litre of the **digestive juices** which break down **carbohydrates**, **proteins** and **fats** in the small intestine. It also produces two **hormones** – insulin and glucagon – that control the amount of sugar in the blood. Insulin is produced when there is too much sugar in the blood, and glucagon when there is too little. A diabetic person is one whose pancreas does not make enough insulin.

▲ Diabetics inject themselves regularly with the insulin which their bodies need but cannot produce.

Did you know?

You could live without most of your stomach but you could not survive without your liver. If only part of the liver is removed, however, you will be all right. Even if only a quarter remains, the liver can still function and new cells grow so quickly that within six to eight weeks the whole organ will be as big as before.

In the large intestine

The large **intestine** is about 1.5 to 2 m long and makes a big loop around the small intestine. Unwanted, indigestible parts of food, water and **minerals** from the small intestine pass slowly through it. The mineral salts and much of the water are absorbed into the body and the remaining waste becomes a softish solid, called **faeces**. This is stored in the **rectum** until it is expelled from the body through the **anus**.

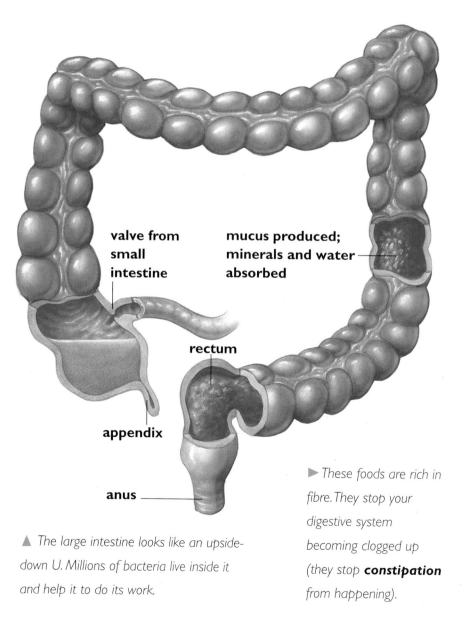

valve from
small
intestine

mucus produced;
minerals and water
absorbed

rectum

appendix

anus

▲ *The large intestine looks like an upside-down U. Millions of bacteria live inside it and help it to do its work.*

▶ *These foods are rich in fibre. They stop your digestive system becoming clogged up (they stop* **constipation** *from happening).*

Water

The fact that water is re-absorbed into the body saves you having to drink so much. Not all the water is absorbed, however. About three-fifths of faeces is water. Drinking plenty of liquid helps to prevent constipation. This is when the faeces become too dry and hard and they are difficult to expel. **Diarrhoea** occurs when the waste passes through the large intestine so quickly there is not enough time for the water to be absorbed. If this happens it is essential to drink extra liquid to replace the water that is lost.

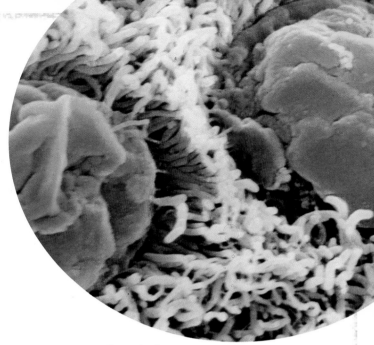

▲ These **cells** in the large intestine absorb water and make **mucus**.

Fibre and bacteria

Much of the undigested food is parts of plants called fibre or roughage. It might seem surprising, but the more fibre you eat, the better the digestive system works. Fibre helps to prevent constipation and diseases such as bowel cancer. Faeces also contain mucus, dead cells from the **gut** lining and millions of **bacteria**, most of which are also dead.

Did you know?

The appendix is a dead-end in the digestive system. It appears to have no use at all, but human beings are not the only ones to have it. Monkeys, apes and rodents have it too. Although the appendix is useless, it can be dangerous. If it becomes inflamed, it causes terrible pain and must be removed in a simple operation.

Kidneys and bladder

You have two **kidneys**, one on each side of the body, just below the ribs. They do two main jobs. They filter the blood to remove poisonous waste (**urea**) and they remove extra water from the blood. The urea and water form **urine** which drains into the **bladder**. It is stored in this stretchy, muscular bag until you get rid of it when you urinate, or pee.

A million filters

As the body's **cells** burn up food and energy, they produce waste (like a car's exhaust). The waste from **carbohydrates** and **fats** is water and carbon dioxide, which is breathed out through the **lungs**. The waste from **protein**, however, is turned into urea by the **liver**. It is carried in the blood to the kidneys.

Inside each kidney there are millions of tiny, twisting tubes and capillaries (very fine blood vessels). The blood passes through this network, where it is filtered. The purified blood is re-absorbed into the body. The urea and any unwanted water are left behind and these trickle down into the bladder.

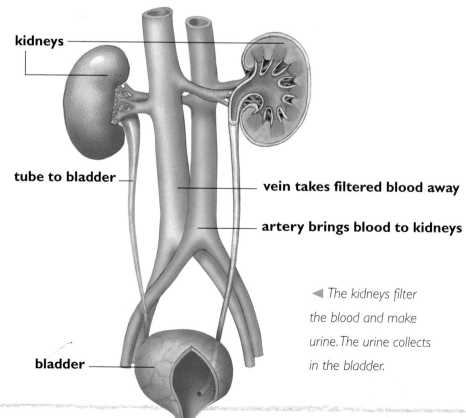

kidneys

tube to bladder

vein takes filtered blood away

artery brings blood to kidneys

bladder

◀ The kidneys filter the blood and make urine. The urine collects in the bladder.

Water control

The kidneys control how much water is lost, so that the body retains just the right amount. They filter about a litre and a half of blood every minute, but make only about 2 litres of urine a day. The more you drink, the more you urinate. But if you get very hot and sweat a lot, you urinate less, because the extra water is then being lost through the skin. A **valve** (or **sphincter**) at the bottom of the bladder stops the urine escaping, but when the bladder is nearly full your brain realizes that you need to empty it. You can then decide when to relax the valve and release the urine.

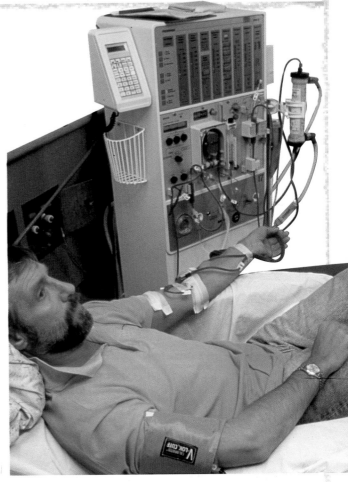

▲ Some people's kidneys do not work properly. Instead this huge machine filters their blood every few days.

Did you know?

Most of your body – about seven-tenths of your weight – is water. Four-fifths of the blood is water, and three-quarters of muscle is water. Your bones are one-quarter water. No wonder water is so important to the body! Most of your food is water too – nine-tenths of fruit and vegetables.

◀ A magnified photograph showing the inside of a kidney.

27

Healthy eating

Food can be unhealthy in two quite different ways. If it contains germs, or if germs get into your **stomach**, you can become ill. Contaminated food can make you sick, give you stomach pains or **diarrhoea**. Your diet is the kind of food you usually eat. If your diet is unhealthy, your body will not work as well as it should, and, over the years, you will get different kinds of diseases.

Hygiene

Food should be kept clean and stored properly. Even food kept in the fridge should usually be eaten within a few days. All food can contain germs. Thorough cooking kills most germs and the stomach juices will kill the rest, provided there are not too many. It is also important to make sure your hands are clean before you eat.

A balanced diet

If you eat a reasonable amount of a variety of foods, you are eating a balanced diet. Doctors think that people who eat a lot of fatty, salty food, such as crisps and sausages, and not much fruit or fresh vegetables, may be storing up problems for later. In adults, **fat** globules, called cholesterol, can gather in the arteries (blood vessels which carry blood away from the heart) and may cause **heart** attacks.

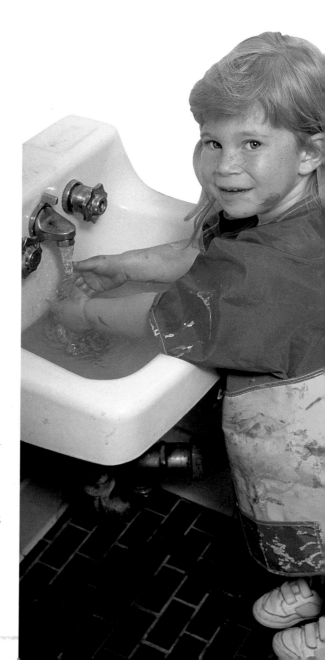

Food and energy

If we eat more fat than we need, the body stores it under the skin. We all need some fat to keep us warm, but too much extra weight puts an extra strain on the heart. It can, however, be more dangerous to be too thin than too fat. The body needs a good supply of food to give you the energy to enjoy yourself and to learn at school. The energy value of food is measured in calories and the actual number of calories you need each day varies according to your age, height and sex, and how much exercise you are getting.

◀ It is important to wash your hands after using the toilet and before eating. Germs on your hands can easily get onto your food and make you ill.

▲ This man is jogging to help avoid becoming overweight. The best way for overweight people to lose weight is to eat less fat and to exercise more.

Did you know?

The heaviest person ever recorded weighed over 363 kg when he died in 1983. He was Jon Minnoch who lived in Washington State in the United States. He weighed nearly five times the North American average weight of 76 kg. Some wrestlers weigh over 220 kg, three times as much as most other men.

Glossary

Acid A sour-tasting substance which can burn skin and corrode (wear down) metals. The mouth and stomach produce acidic juices to help digest food.

Alimentary canal The long tube that joins the mouth to the anus. It consists of the oesophagus, the stomach, and the small and large intestines. It allows food to pass slowly through the body, while the nutrients are digested. Only the waste reaches the anus, at the end of the large intestine.

Alkaline Which neutralizes an acid. The first part of the small intestine, the duodenum, is supplied with alkaline digestive juices.

Amino acids The basic building-blocks that make up proteins.

Antiseptic A substance which fights bacteria or helps to prevent bacterial infection.

Anus The valve or sphincter muscle at the end of the alimentary canal that controls when faeces are released from the rectum.

Appendix A small, dead-end branch at the start of the large intestine.

Bacteria Single, living cells that function independently. They are so small that we can see them only through a microscope. There are millions of bacteria in the mouth and other parts of the body. Most are harmless, but some can cause disease.

Bile A juice which is made in the liver and stored in the gall bladder. It is released into the duodenum, to break down fats into tiny droplets.

Bladder A stretchy, muscular bag that stores urine before it is expelled from the body.

Bolus A packet of food pushed by the tongue into the oesophagus.

Carbohydrates Substances found in food such as bread, rice, pasta, potatoes and sugar, which provide the body with a source of energy. During digestion, the starch in carbohydrates is broken down into simple sugars.

Cell This is the smallest living unit. Each part of the body is built up of a different kind of cell. Each cell has a nucleus which controls what it does and each cell is surrounded by a membrane (similar to a skin).

Chemical reaction A process of change in which the molecules of two or more substances combine to form new substances.

Chyme Food that has been turned into a liquid in the stomach.

Constipation This is when faeces are dry, hard and difficult to expel.

Diaphragm A sheet of muscles below the lungs which contracts and relaxes to make you breathe air in and out.

Diarrhoea This is when faeces are too liquid.

Digest/Digestion To break up/the breaking up of food into smaller molecules that can be absorbed into the blood and used by the body.

Digestive juices Liquids made by glands and released into the alimentary canal to break down food. Digestive juices contain enzymes and may be acidic, alkaline or neutral.

Digestive system All the parts of the body which are used to digest food.

Duodenum The first part of the small intestine. Juices from the liver and pancreas break down food which has passed into the duodenum from the stomach.

Enzymes Proteins made by the body which allow chemical reactions, such as the breaking down of food, to take place quickly without themselves being changed.

Epiglottis A flap in the pharynx that closes off the windpipe to the lungs.

Faeces Softish solid waste expelled from the body through the anus.

Fats Substances found in some foods which the body uses as a source of energy. For example, foods such as eggs, milk, cheese, meat and vegetable oils contain fats which provide a concentrated source of energy.

Gall bladder A small bag in which bile is stored before being released into the duodenum.

Gastric juices Juices produced by the lining of the stomach. They include enzymes and hydrochloric acid which break down food.

Gland An organ of the body which makes special substances such as hormones or digestive juices.

Gut See **Intestines**.

Heart An organ within the chest which pumps blood through the blood vessels to all the body's living cells.

Hormones Chemicals produced by some of the glands which are carried round in the blood and help to control many of the body's processes. Insulin, for example, is a hormone which controls the amount of sugar in the blood.

Ileum The third and last part of the small intestine.

Intestines The long tube (also known as the gut) which connects the stomach to the anus. It consists of two parts – the small intestine and the large intestine.

Jejunum The middle part of the small intestine.

Kidneys A pair of organs which filter blood to remove poisonous waste and produce urine.

Liver An organ of the body which processes digested food molecules and other chemicals in the blood. It is the largest organ in the body.

Lungs Two organs within the chest cavity which are used in breathing. When air is breathed into the lungs, the blood there absorbs oxygen from the air and releases carbon dioxide to be breathed out.

Minerals/Mineral salts Chemicals, such as calcium and phosphorus, which the body needs to stay healthy.

Molecule The smallest part of a substance which can exist by itself and keep the properties of the substance. If a complex molecule is broken down it becomes two or more simpler substances.

Mucus Slimy liquid produced by particular parts of the body.

Muscle A bundle of fibres which contract (shorten and get thicker) to produce movement.

Nutrients The parts of food which the body needs for energy or to build new cells.

Oesophagus The tube that links the mouth with the stomach.

Organ A part of the body, such as the heart, which does a particular job. The stomach, intestines, pancreas and liver are the main digestive organs.

Palate The roof of the mouth, hard at the front, soft at the back.

Pancreas A large gland which produces enzymes to help digest fats and digestive juices. Juices from the pancreas are released into the duodenum. The pancreas also makes insulin which controls the amount of sugar in the blood.

Peristalsis The contractions of the muscles of the oesophagus and intestines which move food through the digestive system. The contractions pass like a wave along the tubes.

Pharynx The back of the throat, passing into the oesophagus.

Protein A substance found in some foods which our bodies need to grow new cells and replace old ones. Protein consists of carbon, hydrogen, oxygen and nitrogen. Parts of the body, such as muscles, are made of protein.

Rectum The final part of the large intestine, before the anus.

Sphincter See **Valve**.

Stomach A muscular bag below the chest in which swallowed food is stored for a few hours while it is churned around and mixed with acidic digestive juices.

Urea Substance which when mixed with water in the kidneys forms urine. Waste protein from the cells is made into urea in the liver and carried in the blood to the kidneys.

Urine The liquid formed by the kidneys from urea and surplus water, stored in the bladder, and expelled as urine.

Valve A device which allows movement in one direction only. There is a round valve, called a sphincter, where one part of the alimentary canal joins the next part.

Villi Tiny finger-like projections about 0.5–1 mm long in the ileum lining which absorb nutrients into the blood.

Vitamins Chemicals that the body needs to stay healthy.

Index